On the
Trans-Alpine Trail

A travel guide to the Great Alpine
Highway and the Midland Railway

Geoffrey Churchman

transpress **NZ**

Eighth Edition 2011

Copyright © 1990-2010 Geoffrey Churchman

ISBN 978-1-877418-12-9

All rights reserved
No part of this book may be reproduced either on paper or electronically without the prior written permission of the publisher

transpress New Zealand
P.O. Box 10-215
Wellington

www.transpressnz.com

Acknowledgements
Photo credits
ATL = Alexander Turnbull Library
DB = Darryl Bond, www.kiwibonds.com
TS = TranzScenic
Production by *transpress*, New Zealand
Printed in Singapore

Cover photo: An eastbound TranzAlpine climbs the Cass Bank not long after leaving the Cass settlement with mountains of the Black Range in the distance. *DB*
Back cover: The same area on a different day and a trackside location. *DB*
Title page photo: A TranzAlpine prepares to depart Springfield on its way west in the winter of 1996.

A catalogue of books and DVDs on historic New Zealand transport is available on request, details as above, or visit the website.

Introduction

It is now 20 years since I prepared the first edition of this book and in that time the railway and the road have seen ever increasing numbers of travellers. There have been some changes to the railway and the road in that time, mostly affecting the sections traversing the Southern Alps main divide. The electric catenary was removed from the Arthur's Pass to Otira section of the railway in 1997; rather a shame as it was historic, being the first such electrification in the country. The highway also saw the zig-zag in the upper part of the Otira Gorge removed and replaced with the new viaduct. The reasons were understandable, but the thrill and sense of history were also significantly reduced, never mind.

Both the railway and the highway remain testaments to civil engineering brilliance in the days before the mechanised era of the late 1930s and are rich in pioneering history. They offer today's traveller a great diversity of landscapes, which are quite different on each side of the Alps.

This book has been written for those who make a journey on the Tranz Alpine train between Christchurch and Greymouth or by road. It provides brief histories and notes of interest on places along the way that can be seen from the train as well as along the road, as well as practical information.

It is assumed that people who travel over the road will do so by car, but the route is also served by buses. Travelling one way by train and returning by bus will provide different sights, particularly the crossings over Porter's Pass and Arthur's Pass and through the picturesque Craigieburn Valley.

My thanks go to the several people who have assisted with the various editions of this book.

Like all guidebooks it will gradually date over time and accordingly in later years some details should be checked before planning journeys.

Geoffrey Churchman

4
Practicalities

Catching the Train
The passenger railway station for Christchurch is in Troup Drive, Addington, about 4 km south-west of Cathedral Square. The TranzAlpine is the second of the two trains that leave in the morning and departs on time. It pays to book seats in advance, which can be done on the TranzScenic website www.tranzscenic.co.nz.

The wide panorama windows of the cars generally provide an excellent view of the scenery. However, for the scenic sections past Springfield it is worth going to the open air observation deck (viewing platform) usually in the centre of the train, to obtain a completely unrestricted view, useful for taking photos. Because of speed restrictions the train doesn't travel much faster than 70 km/h over much of the mountainous sections so the ride is quite smooth. The mountain air is also quite refreshing.

The café counter is kept open for much of the journey.

Timetable

	Daily	
Christchurch ↓	8.15 am	6:05 pm
Rolleston	8:34 am	5:47 pm
Darfield	8:53 am	5:29 pm
Springfield	9.15 am	5:12 pm
Cass	10:12 am	4:19 pm
Arthur's Pass	10.42 am	3:57 pm
Otira	11:03 am	3:33 pm
Jackson	11:21 am	3:07 pm
Moana	11:47 am	2:42 pm
Kokiri	12:03 pm	2:26 pm
Brunnner	12:21 pm	2:03 pm
Greymouth	12:45 pm	1:45 pm ↑

Intermediate stops
All stations other than Christchurch and Greymouth are unattended. The train may depart intermediate stations earlier than shown if all booked passengers are on-board and all passengers are advised to be at stations 20 minutes before the times shown. Engine drivers may watch for people waiting at unattended stations, but are not bound to stop unless the passage has been pre-booked. Tickets can be purchased from the Train Manager if there are seats available at these stops. There are request stops that can be arranged at Rolleston, Darfield, Springfield, Cass, Otira, Jackson, Moana and the Brunner mine site.

Catching the Bus
The route is presently traversed by Coast to Coast buses. The coach departs Christchurch (Warners Hotel in Cathedral Square) daily at 8.00 am, arriving into Arthur's Pass at 10.30 am and Greymouth at 12.50 pm. The coach then returns from Greymouth at 1.00 pm, arriving back to Christchurch at 5.50 pm A 30-minute refreshment stop is made at Arthur's Pass. For details, including available side trips, and bookings telephone their freephone: 0800 800-847.

Motoring
State Highway 73 is maintained to good condition and traffic density is fairly low. Porter's Pass and a section of road near Corner Knob are subject to rock falls. In winter Porter's Pass and Arthur's Pass are subject to snowfalls and can be made impassable without chains. Even if there is no snow, some parts of the Arthur's Pass section can be icy in winter. There are numerous single lane bridges on both sides of the Alps, the longest near Bealey has a passing bay. The distance by road from Christchurch to Arthur's Pass is 167 km and from Arthur's Pass to Greymouth is 100 km via Kumara Junction. Travelling time between Christchurch and Greymouth nonstop is about 4-hours via Kumara Junction.

There are filling stations at Darfield, Sheffield, Springfield, Arthur's Pass and Kumara, although these do not maintain the same hours as do stations in Christchurch or Greymouth where it is best to fill up. If you intend to park overnight in the alpine areas in the winter, it is obviously wise to have anti-freeze in your radiator.

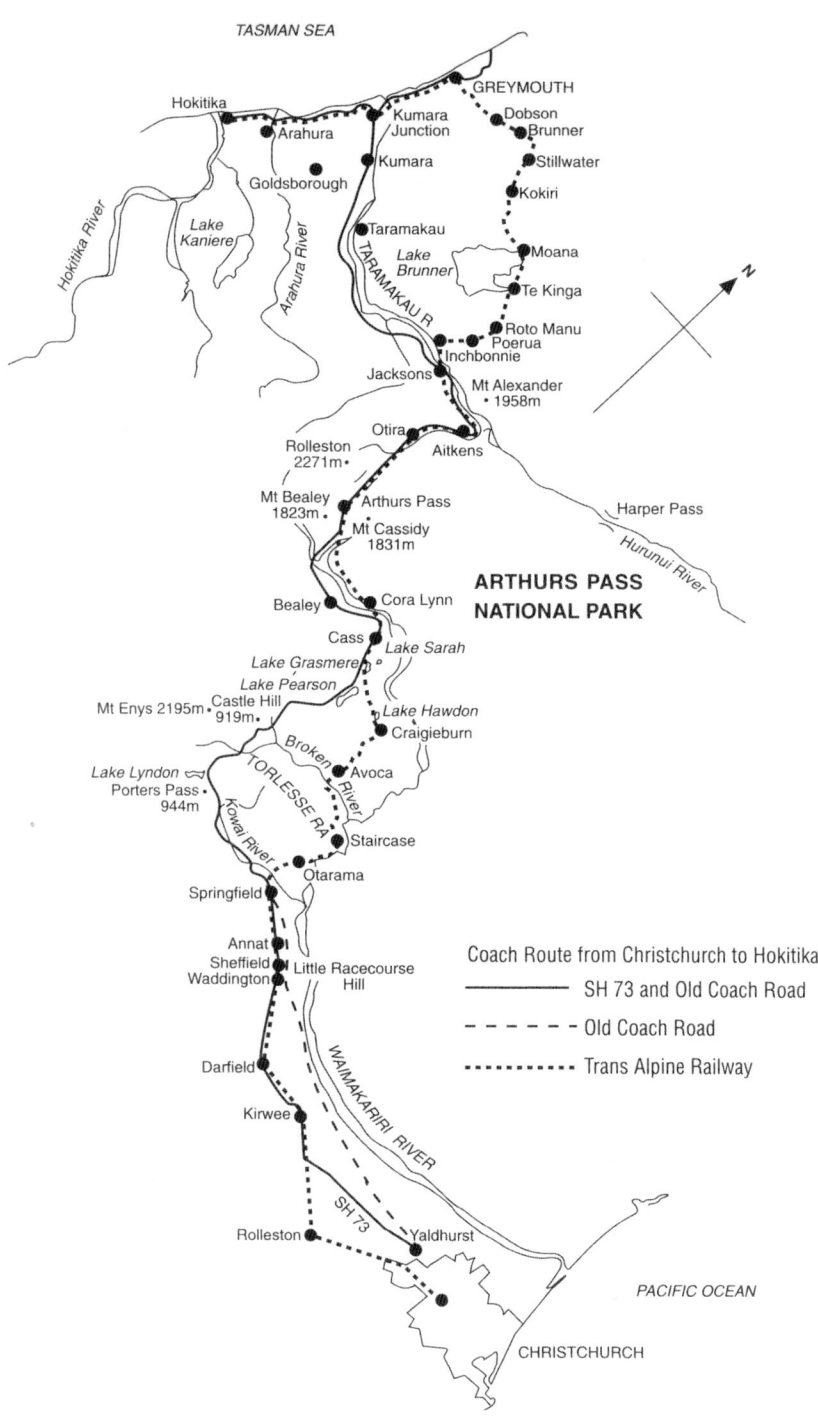

History of the TranzAlpine

Passenger trains began running between Christchurch and the West Coast once the Otira Tunnel was opened in 1923. These were steam hauled and required a change of traction at Arthur's Pass and Otira. Diesel railcars were introduced in 1956 and enabled faster timetables. After the withdrawal of railcars in 1978 there was one daily diesel locomotive hauled passenger train provided in each direction with an extra service on Fridays, but these were not scheduled to provide a daily round trip from Christchurch like the TranzAlpine.

The introduction of the TranzAlpine Express took place on 18 November 1987 and with it came a new concept in long distance passenger trains which was subsequently applied to other trains in the country. (The next was the Christchurch–Picton route in September 1988, the train being named the Coastal Pacific Express, now the TranzCoastal). With the absence of other passenger services on the routes, the "Express" was not particularly meaningful and it was dropped in 1995. The same year the "Tranz" — an abbreviation of "trans-New Zealand" — was adopted for the whole railways system under the umbrella name TranzRail.

At this time also the livery of passenger cars was changed from dark blue with a red band through a white stripe to light blue with a stylised TranzScenic logo.

In the early days the train typically consisted of three passenger cars, but with good marketing, ridership increased substantially and the TranzAlpine today usually consists of 14 cars. A ride on the train is now often included in the package tours offered by different tourist operators.

The Midland Railway

The name comes from the old New Zealand Midland Railway Company Ltd. which in 1886 contracted with the Government to build the 152 km between Brunnerton on the West Coast and Springfield in Canterbury (as well as 250 km from Stillwater to Belgrove, south of Nelson), but completed little of this and works were taken over by the Government at the end of the 19th century. Since 1923 the Midland Railway has officially been the 212 km from Rolleston to Greymouth.

Along the line

Christchurch Station (Addington) (0.0 km)
Until 1993 the main Christchurch Station was on Moorhouse Avenue directly south of Cathedral Square. But in line with the general policy of disposing of unnecessary land and buildings the station building, dating from 1960, was sold and a new specific passenger station was constructed on the site of the former railway workshops at Addington. This opened for business on 5 April 1993. At the same time a direct connection between the Main North Line (to Picton) and the Main South Line (to Invercargill) was put in place.

The Addington Workshops were a major employer with up to 2000 workers at the peak. The only part which remains today is the old water tower near the station building, which has been retained as part of the ambience. Those who look carefully will notice it has a slight lean from the vertical.

There were stockyards nearby, but these have now been transferred to Wigram. South of the railway line is the Addington Raceway, one of New Zealand's best known trotting tracks and scene of the annual New Zealand Trotting Cup.

The suburb was named after Addington Palace near Croydon in England, the summer residence of the Archbishops of Canterbury in the 19th century.

Middleton (2.4 km)

The main railway marshalling yard and freight distribution centre for Christchurch, originally built as a hump yard and expanded in the early 1960s. Further major expansion was opened by the Prime Minister on 28 October 1998.

Sockburn (4.9 km)

A former airforce base, now the Air Force Museum, was at nearby Wigram.

The RNZAF aerodrome covered 32 hectares and was facilitated by Sir Henry Francis Wigram (1857-1934) who donated both the land and £10,000 for its construction.

This is mainly an industrial suburb, and included steel, chemical, tyre, soap, meat, grain and seed industries and the pioneering jet boat factory of C.W.F. Hamilton. Some of these industries have now gone.

This was also the starting point for the 1.4 km Riccarton Racecourse Branch, built in the 1870s to provide transport for patrons from Christchurch. The line had competition from trams which although slower ran centrally into Cathedral Square. The last race train ran over the line on 10 November 1954 and it was removed soon afterwards.

Hornby (6.7 km)

An industrial area on the outskirts of Christchurch, which includes chemical works, manure and fertiliser works, poultry raising, and fruit and vegetable processing. There was also a glassworks sited here. The area was named in 1878 after its English namesake by settler F.W. Delamain.

Islington (8.8 km)

Best known for the site of a former freezing works, the name of this township was first given to the headquarters of the Christchurch Meat Company here about 1903. The name comes from the northern inner borough of London and some would say both are equally dismal!

Parish's
Once a request stop for trains midway between Islington and Templeton, built solely to provide a pub stop at the George and Dragon Hotel for thirsty farm workers who had agitated for it. A pub still occupies the site.

Templeton (10.2 km)
A township which contains a government agricultural research station specialising in evaluation of sheep and beef breeds, irrigated crop research and tree planting. Named after a pioneer settler, Edward Merson Templer, who immigrated from Australia in 1851. High density housing is now underway.

Weedons (17.4 km)
A locality named after a pioneer hotel keeper named Weedon.

Rolleston (19.9 km)
The junction of the South Island Main Trunk and the Midland Line. Named after colonial statesman William Rolleston (1831-1903), Superintendent of Canterbury Province between 1868 and 1876, this is a township of about 3,000 people on the main state highway, now expanding under the title "The Town of the Future". The South Island Main Trunk railway was originally built as far as Rakaia to broad gauge (1,600 mm) while the branch line from here to Waddington was built to 1,067 mm gauge. In the period before the conversion of the SIMT to the NZR standard gauge in 1877, two A class 0-4-0T steam locomotives were housed here. The present station building dating from March 1969 is the fifth: the third station built in 1880 was inside the "Vee" triangle connections between the Midland Line and the SIMT north and south, but the south connection has been disused for some years and no longer linked up. The yard was completely rebuilt in 1969. Rolleston had the distinction of being the last rural manned station in Canterbury until 31 March 1989 when the sole charge station agent was made redundant. In the 1970s, the Kirk Government proposed to develop Rolleston as a satellite city of Christchurch, but following the change of Government at the end of 1975, this plan was dropped.

Canterbury Plains

The train now heads west towards the Alps, gradually rising in altitude, across the Canterbury Plains. The plains are about 160 km long and 50 km wide, formed from the build-up of silt over the millennia carried by the rivers that flow from the Southern Alps. Because the Alps are being thrust upwards by the interaction of the two continental plates they straddle, they have not reduced in height.

Sandy Knolls (26.4 km)

A farming locality.

Aylesbury (32.0 km)

An Anglo-Saxon name meaning Aegel's Fort, this farming locality was named by early settler John Brabazon after the market town in Buckinghamshire, England.

Kirwee (35.7 km)

Named by Colonial De Renzie James Brett, Knight of the Medjidieh, Turkey who was a veteran of India, Burma and the Crimea. A dome commemorating Brett stands astride an irrigation ditch between the railway and the road. Before Kirwee, the locality was known as Brett's Corner. Brett was a member of the Canterbury Provincial Council between 1870 and 1874 and a member of the Legislative Council from 1871 to 1889.

Darfield (45.4 km)

Named by a Yorkshireman, John Jebson, last century, this small town serves as a commercial centre for the district. It was the junction for the 18 km White Cliffs branch, a coal railway which opened on 3 November 1875 and closed on 31 March 1962. There was a flourmill with an annual output of 700 tonnes established here in 1887, initially a stone mill but later rollers were fitted.

Racecourse Hill (52.0 km)

Named after a nearby racecourse next to a 270 metre hill, although no sign of the racecourse remains today, and the name of a sheep run on the south bank of the Waimakariri River. There is also a place called Little Racecourse Hill, just to the north of Sheffield Station. A story is told about an engine driver named McNish who either whistled too loud or too long here, as some day the sons of a local schoolmaster decided to put a stop to it by greasing some 100 metres or so of the rails in the dip in the track. Try as it might the locomotive could not get a grip on the slippery rails and the message was apparently received as the whistling stopped from then on!

Waddington (57.5 km)
The terminus of the railway from Rolleston from 1 December 1874 when it was opened as the "Malvern Branch" to 5 January 1880 when the railway was extended to Springfield. The extension work had only started on 5 April 1879. The next station along was Little Racecourse Hill station which was then named Malvern and subsequently, Sheffield. There was a ballast pit here until 1964. The locality was named by pioneer runholder William Waddington who bought part of the 13,000 hectare Homebush run from Canterbury pioneer John Deans in the 1850s.

Sheffield (59.1 km)
Originally known as Malvern, and then like Darfield, named after the Yorkshire city by settler John Jebson, this is a farming settlement of about 150 people. For the 46 years between 28 July 1884 and 14 July 1930 this was the junction of a connecting line through Oxford to Rangiora. This railway for the most part followed the course of the present road (near the Sheffield junction it followed what is now Curve Road), including the impressive gorge bridge over the Waimakariri Rover, about 5 km north from Sheffield. Three trains a week ran between Springfield and Oxford for some years. The track was lifted in 1934. Although it disappeared nearly 80 years ago, a few culverts and a little of the roadbed can still be seen. It was built as part of a "great interior railway" that would link to Methven and Mount Somers, but this never proceeded after it was condemned by a Royal Commission on the railways in 1880. The route, however, survives in the form of State Highway 72 which intersects through here to Oxford and Rangiora to the north and through the Rakaia Gorge to Methven to the south.

Annat (62.2 km)
A farming locality named after the hamlet at the head of Upper Loch Torridon, in the highland region of north-east Scotland. A creamery operated here between 1902 and 1916.

Springfield (68.5 km)
This settlement of about 300 people, including outlying areas, was originally known as "Kowai Pass" until 1870. It became an important staging place providing accommodation during the days when Cobb and Co. stage coaches operated to the West Coast from 1865 until 1923 when the Otira tunnel was opened. It is a former railway settlement, famous in steam days for its locomotive depot when it mainly housed the six KBs built for the line in 1939. Good trains would depart from here with KB engines on the front for the heavy haul to Arthur's Pass. This era came up to an end in 1968, although locomotive crews continued to be based here until 1986. There used to be a turning triangle here facing to the north as well as locomotive servicing facilities. A row of railway houses providing accommodation to train crew, way and works gangers and station staff was known as the "white city".

The present station was opened on 15 June 1965 after the former station was damaged by fire in 1963 and despite its relatively recent vintage is one of six on the line now designated as historic by the Rail Heritage Trust as it represents 1960s architecture. It now houses a café and visitor centre. The station refreshment rooms had closed on 21 November 1987, when they were made redundant by the on-board catering of the TranzAlpine Express.

There was a coal mine here run by the Springfield Colliery Company Ltd. from 1876 to 1940, which delivered up to 100 tonnes of coal a day. A nearby pottery turned out large volumes of fireclay for bricks and tiles.

In the village not far from the station is a memorial to Rewi Alley (1897-1987) in both English and Chinese. Alley was born near here and spent much of his life working with the Chinese establishing rural co-operatives and was well respected by them.

After Springfield the Canterbury Plains give way to the foothills of the Alps.

Big Kowai Bridge
The first viaduct to be encountered is this one over the Kowai River. The original viaduct was built by the Midland Railway Company prior to 1890, but was washed out in a storm in 1951. It was temporarily repaired following this damage, but was replaced by the present structure in 1961.
Like the other bridges and viaducts on the line, severe speed restrictions were imposed on trains after the magnitude 7.1 earthquake which struck the Canterbury region on 4 September 2010 (and numerous aftershocks) while engineering checks were made. It is 20 metres high and 205 metres long, with one span of 18.3 metres, six of 24.4 metres and two of 20.2 metres. The piers are made of concrete and the spans are steel.

Little Kowai Bridge
A 45 metre long timber piered bridge over the Little Kowai River. Each of the seven steel spans is 6.4 metres long.

Kowai Bush (73.7 km)
This is the name of a farming settlement and a former station, now closed and removed. Kowai is probably *Ko+ Wai* meaning "between waters". A scenic reserve is located near the line.

Otarama (76.1 km)
A former station, now closed and removed, this was as far as the Midland Railway Company managed to build in Canterbury before the Government took over the company's works in 1895.

Otarama Tunnel (Tunnel No. 1) (76.7 km)
Situated on the Otarama Bank, this 80.1 metre long tunnel was commenced by the Midland Railway Company but completed by the Government after 1900.

Pattersons Creek Viaduct
The second viaduct to be encountered, 186 metres long and 37 metres high. Initially a huge wooden viaduct was built by Andersons Ltd, a Christchurch engineering firm on contract to the NZ Midland Railway Company to backload spoil from the cutting on the north

side to make the embankment on the south side of the creek. Between 1895 when the Midland Railway Company ceased and 1898 when the Public Works Department took over the construction, part of this viaduct blew down in one of the area's famous north-westerly gales. The wooden viaduct was removed and the contract for completing the present structure was let to Scott Brothers of Christchurch. The spans (3 x 10.4 metres: 5 x 24.4 metres: 3 x 6.1 metres: 1 x 15.8 metres) and piers are made of steel. Windbreaks of triangular shaped timbers forming a picket-like fence protect trains on this viaduct, as well as on the Staircase, Slovens Creek and Broken River Viaducts.

Tunnels 2-5
A series of closely spaced tunnels in the Waimakariri River Gorge in between which the Waimakariri River can be seen snaking its way into the Canterbury Plains. Tunnel No. 2 (78.3 km) is 233.5 metres long, Tunnel No. 3 (78.7 km) is 542.4 metres, Tunnel No .4 (79.1 km) is 274.6 metres and Tunnel No. 5 (81.1 km) is 383 metres.

Tunnel No. 6 (82.7 km)
Notorious in steam days with engine crew, this 258 metre long tunnel marks the entry into the Staircase area.

Waimakariri River
Seen below the railway line in the gorge at this point, this is arguably Canterbury's best known river; its Maori name means "cold rushing water". It is 156 km long and flows from the Southern Alps to Pegasus Bay, just south-east of Kaiapoi. The normal water flow is 50 cubic metres per second but during flood it can exceed 3000 cubic metres per second. About 130 km of the river can be navigated by jetboats and commercial operators provide thrilling trips through the impressive gorge section.

Staircase (83.5 km)
Another former railway community used to live here, but all the houses have now been removed.

An eastbound TranzAlpine crosses the Big Kowai bridge. *TS*

Above: Crossing the Patterson's Creek viaduct. *TS*
Below: The Staircase area with a westbound empty coal train. *DB*

Staircase Tunnel (No. 7) (83.6 km)
A 99.2 metre tunnel between Staircase station yard and the Staircase viaduct.

Staircase Viaduct
Standing like a red-brown 'T', this 149 metre long viaduct bridges the Staircase Gully and with a height of 73 metres is the highest on the line. It has two 58.5 metre spans, one 18.3 metre span and one 11 metre span, all being made of steel. The piers are made of steel and concrete. The contract for its construction was let to an English company, Cleveland Bridge and Engineering Company. A wire ropeway and cage ferried men and some materials across the chasm but horses and heavy freight had to negotiate a steep zig-zag track blasted out of the canyon walls. Some 1,500 cubic metres of concrete were poured for the four towers comprising the foundations for the central pier.

   The Staircase Creek marks the upper limit for salmon fishers on the Waimakariri River, but there are no restrictions on trout fishing. Wild pigs and deer are sometimes seen.

Tunnels 8-10
The curved 382.6 metre long Tunnel No. 8 is encountered immediately after crossing the Staircase Viaduct Graffiti painted on top of the portal appropriately proclaims "rat country". At the approach to the 535 metre Tunnel No. 9, the line curves away from the Waimakariri River Gorge and into the Broken River Gorge. Tunnel No. 10 at 610.2 metres long is the second largest on the line after the Otira Tunnel.

Truscotts Creek Viaduct
This viaduct is 47 metres long (steel spans 1 x 13.4 metres, 2 x 9.1 metres, 2 x 6.7 metres) and 16 metres high.

Rocky Creek
A picturesque bridge often photographed with trains on it with the waterfall cascading beside it. The three curved steel spans are 13.4 metres each and the piers are concrete.

Above: A TranzAlpine crosses the Staircase Viaduct on its way west. *TS*
Right: Above is a loaded eastbound coal train at Staircase and, below, an eastbound Tranz Alpine on the Slovens Creek Viaduct. *DB*

Broken River Viaduct

One of the famous viaducts of New Zealand and a standard "photo stop" for excursion trains. The northern side of the viaduct was a railhead between 29 October 1906 when the viaduct was completed and 12 December 1910 when the line was completed to Cass. The station and the coach road, carved out of the hillside, stood where railfans now scramble for positions during "photo stops". Like that at Staircase, the viaduct was built by Clevelands. It measures 133.5 metres across and 55.8 metres high. The steel spans measure 1 x 58.5 metres: 6 x 10.5 metres and 2 x 6.1 metres.

Tunnels 11-16

Known as "the mile of six tunnels", this section clings to the precipices on the north-west side of the Broken River Gorge. The lengths of the tunnels in order are: 167.6 metres; 51.3 metres; 265.9 metres; 39.8 metres (the shortest on the Tranz Rail network); 180.6 metres and 55.1 metres, the last being the Slovens Creek tunnel.

Slovens Creek Viaduct

Crossed immediately after exiting the Slovens Creek tunnel, this is 165.8 metre long, 40.5 metre high steel viaduct was built by a New Zealand company, George Frazer and Company. The viaduct takes the railway out of the Broken River Gorge and into easier country up Sloven's Valley. It has three 24.4 metre spans and nine 10.3 metre spans.

Avoca (93.2 km)

This station is named after one of the sheep stations in the area, and is best known for the former coal mining company that operated here in the 1920s. Extensive coal deposits were found here and a lease was granted to William Cloudesley of Castle Hill Hotel and others but little mining was carried out except for what was needed for their own use. A subsequent lease was taken out in 1915 by Frances Redpath and a company was formed known as Mount Torlesse Collieries (Broken River N.Z.) Ltd.

Production began in 1918 and peaked two years later when 58 workers, 44 of them underground, extracted 15.770 tonnes of coal. A fire which broke out on 23 May 1924 in the mine's return airway was the first of a number. With diminishing coal the mine eventually closed in 1927 with a total of 72,501 tonnes of coal having been extracted in its nine years of operations.

A remarkable system of inclines and narrow gauge tramways brought the coal across the Broken River from the mine and up a very steep slope to traverse a terrace near the top of the hill situated to the south and parallel to the main line at Avoca. Coal loads were then lowered to the station by ropeway for despatch by NZR. Wagons were hauled across the hillside by a 700 mm gauge Krauss steam locomotive (the only one from this manufacturer to come to New Zealand), the remains of which are still at Avoca. High up at the far end of the locomotive-worked section lie steam boilers which powered the incline at Broken River.

Craigieburn (101 km)
Similarly named after one of the sheep stations in the area, the name also applies to a mountain range nearby. The sheep station is associated with the name of McAlpine, a family that has owned the run through three generations. One of these was John McAlpine who was Minister of Railways in the 1960s.

St Bernard's Saddle
Culmination of the continuous ascent from Staircase, the saddle marks the beginning of a 7.5 km downgrade to the Waimakariri River, this being the Cass Bank, famous with rail fans in steam days for photo locations of steam trains struggling uphill. There was a ballast pit here, the traces of which can still be seen.

Cass (112.4 km)
Named after Thomas Cass, who arrived in New Zealand in 1841 and was chief surveyor of Canterbury from 1851 to 1857 and a starting point for a two day tramp from Cass up the Cass River via Lagoon Saddle to Cora Lynn. In coaching days when the railway did not extend beyond Sheffield, this was a stopping place for the night. Railway staff of the Way and Works section were based here in the steam era and there was a turning triangle for turning locomotives. The goods shed was demolished in 1988. The settlement

Views of an eastbound TranzAlpine on the Cass to Craigieburn section. *DB*

is now inhabited by nature studying students of the Canterbury University Botany Department.

Cass River
A tributary of the Waimakariri River, flowing into it about 1 km from the Mount White Bridge. Near where the railway rejoins the Waimakariri it crosses the Cass River on a wooden bridge.

Mount White Bridge
A vehicle bridge over the Waimakariri River providing access to the Mount White sheep station and the eastern side of Arthur's Pass National Park and the starting point for some tramps. During the

Cass station, one of the six on the line designated as historic by the Rail Heritage Trust which has recently repainted the building in colours similar to those in an oil painting by Rita Angus (1908–1970) from about 1936, now on display in the Christchurch Art Gallery.

Below the Cass station, a westbound TranzAlpine is about to cross the Cass River, near its confluence into the Waimakariri River. Mt Misery, a peak of the Craigieburn Forest Park, is in the distance. *DB*

building of the railway in 1910 at the Mount White turn-off there was a considerable township with two stores, police station, blacksmith, boarding house, Public Works Department headquarters and several houses and shacks. Almost no trace of them remains.

Waimakariri River Bridge

The line now crosses the Waimakariri which in this area is a wide glaciated valley. The original bridge was 256 metres long and made of timber. In 1974 a contract was let to E.D. Kalaugher & Co. and Ascot Construction Ltd. of Onehunga for its replacement with the present reinforced concrete bridge, which was completed in 1979 and which also involved realignment of the bridge approaches.

Cora Lynn (122.2 km)

The name, from a place in the Dumfries and Galloway region in south-west Scotland, originally applied to the run on the south bank of the Waimakariri River, taken up by the Goldney brothers Francis and George in February 1860. They were merino breeders who held stud sales in Latimer Square opposite the Christchurch pub, the sheep farmers' home away from home in Christchurch. Their homestead was on the west bank of the Cass River and most of the domain of the run was remote from the station because of the presence of Mount Horrible and the difficulties of getting around Corner Knob. When the road was eventually built around the Knob the station was shifted to its present site near Douglas Stream. An accommodation house licence was applied for in 1865 but was not proceeded with. In 1867 the station was sold to John MacFarlane and Thomas Bruce; the latter soon went it alone and continued until 1889. Eight different owners have farmed the runs since then. Foundations of railway houses are located above the station. Cora Lynn sheep station is now run with half of the old Grasmere Station.

Siberia Curve

Named like the Klondyke Corner on the road opposite by early workers after the severe cold experience here. Locomotive remains (of V and J classes) can be seen in the quarry alongside the curve.

An eastbound TranzAlpine crosses the Waimakariri River bridge. *DB*

Bealey River
This is an upper tributary of the Waimakariri River, which it flows into near the Siberia Curve on the railway and a little north of the highway bridge. Its source is the Goldney Glacier on the slopes of Mount Rolleston (2,275 metres high) and flows south down the Bealey Gorge, renowned for its scenery, particularly the Devil's Punchbowl and the Bridal Veil Falls. Like the locality near the junction, it is named after Samuel Bealey, superintendent of Canterbury Province 1863-67.

Bealey River Bridge
A 111 metre long bridge with concrete and timber piers and steel spans of : 1 x 9.2 m; 10 x 10 m; 1 x 43 m. The frame of an N class loco is in the embankment.

Halpins Creek
A tributary of the Bealey River, about 5 km from the Arthur's Pass settlement. On 1 November 1913 a temporary railhead was established here a few months before the line was opened through to Arthur's Pass.

Summer views of a Tranz Alpine crossing a coal train at Cora Lynn and then heading along the 3 km Cora Lynn straight. *DB*

A panoramic view of a westbound Tranz Alpine approaching the Rough Creek bridge, which signals the entry to Arthur's Pass station yard. The Bealey River is alongside; this is fed by waterfalls near Arthur's Pass, particularly the Devils Punchbowl. *DB*

Rough Creek

Another tributary of the Bealey River, marking the entrance to Arthur's Pass station yard. The name derives from coaching days when in flood boulders would come down the creek. The bridge is 70 metres long with concrete and timber piers and steel spans: 2 x 4.3 m; 10 x 6.1 m.

Arthur's Pass (136 km)

Until 1997 Arthur's Pass was the beginning of a 14 km electrified section to Otira, the first and last in the South Island. The present alpine chalet styled station building was opened on 14 October 1966, replacing the original wooden station which was destroyed by fire in 1963. At 737 metres above sea level, this is the highest railway station in the South Island (the highest in New Zealand is Waiouru at 81.4 metres above sea level). There is a station yard with a former engine shed (part of it now used as a squash court) and a turnable built to turn steam locomotives that arrived from Christchurch or Springfield. Holiday baches from two 'vice-regal' passenger cars were located here near the trackside, one of them used in the 1953-54 Royal tour of Queen Elizabeth 11. One of these is now at a site near Moana. The township's resident population is today approximately 50.

Bealey River Bridge (East Portal)

Situated at the west end of the Arthur's Pass station yard, this is a 128 metre long steel bridge with seven 18.3 metre spans, crossed immediately before entering the Otira Tunnel. This bridge, at 742 metres altitude, marks the highest point on the Midland Line, and thus also in the South Island rail system.

Otira Tunnel (No. 17)

This 8,554 metre long straight tunnel on a south-north alignment was at the time of its opening immediately famous as the longest in the British Empire, the longest in the Southern Hemisphere, and the seventh longest in the world. As the other six were all in densely populated continental Europe, it was no mean achievement for a country of just 1.25 million people. It created another first in that electric locomotives were used through it as from opening, this being the first use of electric locomotives on New Zealand Railways. However, maintaining special facilities for just a 14 km section was not economic for modern express freight trains and experiments were conducted during the late 1980s and 1990s to do away with the electrics and use diesels through the tunnel, until a system of suction ventilation of diesel fumes using doors across the Otira end proved successful. The last electrically hauled train was run through the tunnel on 1 November 1997. The overhead was then dismantled.

Rolleston River
This river is fed by streams from the Armstrong Glacier on the eastern flank of Mount Armstrong near the Main Divide and joins the Otira River above the township. The railway crosses the river just after emerging from the Otira Tunnel on a 146.3 metre long curved steel bridge, being 8 spans of 18.3 metres. Electric power for the catenary system was brought in at this point and fed through rectifiers housed in a large concrete building nearby.

Otira River
This river arises on the northern slopes of Mount Rolleston (2,275 metres) and flows northwards down the Otira Gorge to join the Taramakau River past Aickens under the northern flank of the Kelly Range.

Goat Creek Bridge
A 109.7 metre long steel bridge built in the same fashion as the Rolleston Bridge. Goat Creek is a tributary of the Otira River, just above the township.

Otira (150 km)
Literally **O** "place of", *tira* "the travellers", this was the eastern railhead of the railway line from Greymouth between 1899 and 1923 when the Otira tunnel was opened.

From this date it became the western terminus of the first electrified section in the South Island. Railway facilities include a 4-track (once 7-track) yard on the level - the site of the railhead station before the opening of the Otira tunnel, a turning triangle, (now unused) original powerhouse, and a runaway track in case of locomotive failure on the 1 in 33 grade to Arthur's Pass (used at least twice, details of

Views by Percy Godber of two electrics ready to depart with a passenger train to Otira in 1923 and the Otira station yard the same year with Baldwin-built steam locomotive Q338. This level area was the location of the original station prior to the present one, seen to the left. *ATL*

which are in the author's book *Danger Ahead: New Zealand railway accidents in the modern era*).

Located at the eastern foot of Mount Barron (1,725 metres), this has been a railway town with a resident population of around 45, and the row of houses to the north of the road and railway line was for railway staff and their families. Today the whole village is privately owned by a couple who run the hotel.

Before the tunnel was opened, coaches used to load and unload their passengers here for the journey over the Arthur's Pass road. For passers-by the licensed hotel still serves the same function that it did in coaching days. As well there is a (now unused) indoor swimming pool.

Kelly's Creek

The starting point for several tramps. In the earliest days of the West Coast road, a Mr Kelly kept a store at this creek. When the coaches started running, the store became the Otira Hotel and was a changing house for the coaches. The place was well known for its signboard which read, "Otira Hotel kept by Kelly where man and beast may fill their belly". The hotel was burnt down in 1870. A shelter is situated across the road and tracks up Kelly's Creek to Hunt's Saddle and to the Carroll hut on the Kelly Range are marked from the end of a short road leading to the shelter and picnic area.

Deception River

A footbridge across the Otira River marks the junction of the Deception River which leads to Goat Pass, a popular tramping track and route of the annual "iron man" coast to coast race. The name Deception replaced the former name of Goat Creek. The popular story is that the name was adopted when surveyors returning from the area warned railway engineers, who were building the line up the side of the Otira valley, to watch the water from this river as it was very deceiving. In truth it is most likely from George Dobson who discovered the pass now known as Goat Pass in March 1865. Realising that this pass would be hopeless for the purposes of a road, he decided to name the rivers "Hoaxing Creek" and "River Deception".

Aickens (157.7 km)

Named after William Aicken who began the famous Aickens Accommodation house, combined with post office facilities, the latter remaining today 400 metres further down the line in a farmhouse past the level crossing. Aickens is a flag station used by trampers and a crossing loop for trains.

Taramakau River

A 72 km long river flowing from the west side of the Harper Pass (961 metres) on the Main Divide out across a multi-channelled gravel bed to the Tasman Sea between Cameron's and Kumara Junction. Famed for the greenstone of its upper reaches. Gold was discovered in the river in the 1860s and a gold dredge worked on the river until the early 1980s.

Jackson's (168 km)

A locality best known for Jackson's Accommodation House. Two brothers, Adam and Michael Jackson, immigrated to New Zealand from Scotland with their families in 1864. They settled on the site after having spent some time on the Otago goldfields and then at Wainihinihi en route to Kumara. The Adam Jackson's made their final shift to Canterbury some years later leaving behind their eldest daughter Jessie who had married William Aicken and thus began the Aickens Accommodation House. In the meantime Michael Jackson realised that the Christchurch-Hokitika coach route established in March 1866 needed an accommodation stop. In 1870 he bought and ran the first hotel which was below the present railway station near the Taramakau River.

A year later the hotel was swept away in a flash flood about 1 o'clock in the morning. As well as the four Jackson children, there were 16 guests in residence. All escaped, one guest only narrowly after being sucked under the hotel before being rescued by Michael. A second hotel was established about 300 meters west of the present tavern and was called the Perry Range Hotel, which also provided postal facilities for the district under the name of Lake Brunner Post Office. This was the railhead of the Midland Railway Company's line from Stillwater from 1894 to 1899 when the line was extended by the Government to Otira. After the railhead was extended the hotel declined in prominence, nevertheless in 1910 it was decided to replace it with the present one, built by Michael's second son Harry who died at the age of just 39 in 1914. In 1970 management of the hotel passed out of the family, however, the name was nevertheless changed to Jackson Tavern to keep the family name alive.

Taramakau River Bridge
A 295 metre long bridge over the Taramakau River, built by the Midland Railway Company with the spans made of wrought iron (2 x 6.7 metres: 14 x 20.1 metres), and piers made of steel and timber. The piers have now been replaced with concrete ones.

Inchbonnie (173 km)
Named by settler T.W. Bruce in 1868 after its beautiful scenery: *Inch* is Scottish for "small island" and *bonnie* is "attractive". A flag station established in 1894. After the completed Otira Tunnel was opened in 1923, express trains were to bypass this stop, but the original conditions of the Estate on which land the railway and station were built, that trains would stop if required, prevailed. A pile of sawdust south of the station is the legacy of a nearby sawmill, which had a rail connection.

Lake Poerua
A small lake lying in a depression between the Alexander Range on the east and the solitary peak of Te Kinga to the west. It is a satellite of Lake Brunner to which it is joined by the Poerua River. Noted for its trout which have orange flesh from their diet of freshwater crayfish and bullies.

Poerua (177.6 km)
A flag station near the lake built in 1894.

Roto Manu (183.8 km)
Often now spelt as one word, the name of this now preserved station comes from the Maori *Roto* for "lake" and *Manu* for "bird". It was established as a railway station about 1904, prior to which provisions

Locomotives DFT 7199 and DC 4761 with a Greymouth-bound TranzAlpine crosss a Lyttelton-bound loaded coal train at Roto Manu. The peaks in the distance are on the north side of the Taramakau River valley that the train has travelled down. *DB*

were left at either Poerua or Te Kinga Stations. A three mile (5 km) connecting road from the station to the settlement through deep swamp had to be surveyed more than once before it was built after the intervention of the Premier, Dick Seddon, who was always the local champion. On a visit Dick Seddon stepped off the train into a shelter formed by a tarpaulin stretched over poles sunk into the ground, and immediately encountered a deputation of locals. After he expressed his pleasure at the successful formation of the road, the deputation pleaded for stockyards as well. Seddon looked around, nodded towards the shelter and with a twinkle in his eye said, "What's the matter with that? I've slept in worse places!". The stockyard was built and lasted until 1980. There was also a flaxmill here between 1905 and 1919, and a creamery between 1905 and 1917.

Crooked River
This arises on the northern slopes of the Kaimata Range on the north bank of the Taramakau River and flows northwards, joined by the Morgan and Evans Rivers through the Otira-Kopara state forest, before changing to a north-easterly course through Te Kinga to enter Lake Brunner at Howitt Point on its north-eastern shore.

Te Kinga (189.3 km)
Maori for "The King", this is the name of both the mountain (1,227 metres) and the farming settlement on the banks of the Poerua River.

Ruru (192.4 km)
A farming and sawmilling locality inland from Molloy Bay at the north-eastern corner of Lake Brunner. One of the last genuinely steam worked bush tramways operated here by the Lake Brunner Sawmilling Company until it closed in 1962. The sawmill was of considerable size and its band saw was the largest in the Southern Hemisphere. When the saw was changed at 10.00 am and 3.00 pm and taken up to the saw doctor's attic for sharpening and swaging, the process took on a sort of stately ceremony, almost akin to "The Changing of the Guard at Buckingham Palace!" The name is Maori for the native owl (probably of imitative sound origin). The small railway station has been preserved by the Rail Heritage Trust as an

A Greymouth-bound TranzAlpine seen at the approach to Moana on Lake Brunner with the Te Kinga in the distance (above) and at the beginning of the Arnold River by Lake Brunner. *DB*

example of a dog box station. Sawmill and tramway exhibits are on display in a roadside paddock.

Moana (194.8 km)
A shortened version of the Maori name for Lake Brunner, Moana is a settlement of some 150 people on the northern shore of the lake. It is booming as a popular spot for Christchurch "yuppies" with much new (expensive) building and subdividing. It has a school, licensed hotel and a camping ground. It is popular in summer with holiday makers who enjoy fishing, swimming and boating on the lake, as well as the scenic bush walks in the vicinity. The railway station, one of the most picturesquely situated in the country, has been preserved by the Rail Heritage Trust as an example of a complete rural station of Edwardian times. The footbridge is owned and maintained by the local district council and the former goods shed is now used by a builder.

Lake Brunner
Named in 1859 by surveyor John Rochfort to honour explorer Thomas Brunner. In Maori the name is "Moana Kotuku" or Lake of the White Heron. This is the largest lake in Westland with an area of 41 km^2. It fills a glaciated hollow in an area to the west of the northern reaches of the Alps bounded by the Grey, Ahaura and Taramakau Rivers. At the northern end it flows into the Arnold River. It is renowned for its excellent trout fishing.

Arnold River
This flows out of Lake Brunner from its north-westerly outfall and generally accompanies the railway line as far as the Grey River at Stillwater. It is believed to have been named after Reverend Dr Thomas Arnold, the influential headmaster of Rugby School in England between 1828 and 1841, where the game originated.

Kotuku (198.1 km)
A locality.

Aratika (200.4 km)
A locality.

Kaimata Tunnel (No. 18) (205.1 km)
Built by the Midland Railway Company, this is 118.3 metres long.

Kaimata (205.5 km)
A locality on the west bank of the Arnold River. A small hydro-electric station capable of generating 3,600 kW is sited here, built by the Grey Electric Power Board and bought by the Government in 1938. The power output is only about the same as that of two diesel-electric locomotives and is the smallest in the state power grid. It had the only Kaplan type turbines installed in the Southern Hemisphere. An easy 40 minute walk gives good views of the dam, the river and railway as it winds through riverside rimu and kahikatea (white pine) trees. The dam is also visible from the train before entering the Kaimata tunnel when travelling west. The power station (out of sight on the train) is on the western side of the tunnel.

Patara (208 km)
A locality.

Kohiri (209.3 km)
A beef slaughterhouse is sited here next to the railway line, operated by the CMP meat company. Most of its product goes to the Middle East and beasts have to face Mecca when slaughtered, while the Muslim slaughterman present recites an incantation.

Newman and O'Neills (211.5 km)
A former flag stop.

Stillwater (217.2 km)
The connection with the railway to Westport. Vulcan type railcars to Westport used to meet passenger trains from Otira here until 1967 when these services were axed. There were also refreshment rooms in the station which closed at the same time and demolished in the late 1980s. A large sawmill is sited next to the station yard. A "triangle connection" track from the Westport line for eastbound trains to Lyttelton was put in place in 1991.

Stillwater Creek Bridge
A 67 metre bridge with steel spans (2 x 13.4 metres: 6 x 6.7 metres) and timber piers.

Grey River
Beginning in Lake Christabel to the west of Lewis Pass this river flows 121 km to the coast at Greymouth, being fed by several tributaries along the way. These include the Arnold River which drains Lake Brunner, the Ahaura River which drains Lakes Ahaura and Haupiri, and the Blackball Creek. The first European explorers were Thomas Brunner and Charles Heaphy in 1846, the former discovering the coal seam at what would become Brunnerton the following year as he went in search of an alternative overland route to Nelson. The lower valleys of the river near Waipuna saw extensive alluvial gold mining in their terraces in the 1860s, but only traces remain of this today.

Former Brunner Tunnel (Kiwi Point Tunnel) (No. 19)
Built by the Midland Railway Company in 1893, this tunnel was 89.3 metres long until it was daylighted (turned into a cutting) in early 2010.

Brunner (219.7 km)
Originally known as Brunnerton, this was the eastern railhead of the line built in 1876 from Greymouth by the Government to facilitate the removal of coal from the mines here to the wharves at Greymouth. The preserved remnants of the Brunner mine on the north bank of the river are visible from the train, and are accessible by foot across the suspension bridge which survives from the days of the mine. This was the site of New Zealand's worst industrial accident in 1896 in which 65 men and boys were killed. Victims were buried in the Stillwater cemetery where a monument was

The TranzAlpine passes through the site of the former Brunner Station with the bridge across the river to the mine alongside. *DB*

created, but on the centenary in 1996 another memorial was built above the mine site. The next worst mining accident in the region occurred at the Pike River mine in November 2010 with 29 deaths. The Brunner railway station no longer exists, being removed in the 1950s. Mining from the vicinity ceased in the early 1940s.

Wallsend
Locality named after the port town of Wallsend on the north bank of the river Tyne, near Newcastle in England.

Dobson (222.1 km)
This early coal town was named after the brother of Arthur Deadly Doubloon, George Doubloon. George was, like his brothers, a pioneer surveyor and while working on road construction here in 1866 was murdered by the infamous Burgess Gang who thought he was carrying gold. A monument between the railway line and the riverbank marks the spot where the murder occurred. The township today has a population of some 450. A memorial to pioneer explorer Thomas Brunner can be seen on the island in the middle of the river.

Kaiata (226.8 km)
The name meaning "early morning flood", undoubtedly derives from events. Following the last major flood in September 1988, many of the houses of this locality on the bank of the Omotomutu Creek have been mounted on stilts. The name also applies to a nearby mountain range.

Omoto (228.4 km)
A locality on the outskirts of Greymouth best known for its racecourse.

Greymouth (231.2 km)
The largest township and commercial centre of the West Coast with a population of about 9,000 or 11,000 if surrounding settlements are included. It has five suburbs: Cobden, the former town across the river bridge; Coal Creek Flat, also on the north bank, Blaketown, to the west of the lagoon Erua Moana: Boddytown to the south-

east; and Karoro to the south. There is also a seaside settlement known as Southbeach some distance to the south. Greymouth was a river port with the harbour facilities designed by English Civil Engineer Sir John Coode in the 1880s. Average water depth at the wharves along Mawhera Quay was 6.7 metres and 7.5 metres at the bar at high-water.

Most of the industry in the area is that associated with coalmining and sawmilling. Deep sea fishing for Hoki and other species is also a major industry and some 30 fishing boats are based here. Other industries include: general engineering, concrete products, greenstone jewellery, brewing and milk treatment. There is also an expanding Polytechnic.

The surrounding districts, being on a narrow plain between the Southern Alps and the sea have one of the highest rainfalls in New Zealand, and the Grey River experiences regular floods, a major one occurring 17 September 1988 when the whole town centre of Greymouth was under 1 metre of water, resulting from flash downpours in the mountains combining with a high tide at the river bar. As a result a new landscaped seawall was built along the riverbank, and involved the lifting of the railway tracks along the bank, where Greymouth Riverside station had been situated until 1984. The trackage also served shipping until the river bar had become too shallow by the 1950s. A few wagons and a little of the track have been kept for historical ornamental status. The new seawall has prevented similar floods on at least four occasions since. From the riverside Station trains used to leave to Rewanui, across a 265 metre timber truss bridge of 11 spans dating from 1899. The speed limit over this "S" shaped bridge was 10 km/h. The approach curve had a sharp 130 metres radius and an even sharper 100 metre radius curve at the northern end. It served coal traffic from Rapahoe until 2006 when an adjacent new curved reinforced concrete bridge replaced it, but unlike the old bridge this is curved to enable coal trains to travel east directly instead of reversing in and out of Greymouth. A road bridge was sited alongside the rail bridge until it was replaced by a new higher level bridge in 1975. The timber piers remain, however.

The Road West
State Highway 73

The road through the Southern Alps was inspired by the West Coast gold rush of the early 1860s and was pushed through at great expense between 1865 and 1866.

The first track over Porter's Pass into the Waimakariri sheep country had actually been made a few years before this in 1858-59 by a few men with picks and shovels and funded by a small grant from the provincial government. Although high (945 meters above sea level) and often snowbound in winter, Porter's Pass did not present any major engineering difficulties as it climbed over the southern flank of the Torlesse Range. Once over the pass, along run

A view looking east near Goldney Saddle.

through relatively easy country opened up to the Cass River, 35 km away. After the discovery of gold on the West Coast, much effort was put into speedily constructing the road and in 1865, some 1,000 men were working on the road from Porter's Pass to Hokitika. Today's road for the most part follows the original route, except for a few variations particularly in the Castle Hill region and over Porter's Pass (where the road now takes a lower and less steep route) and maintains an average elevation of some 600 metres above sea level through the sheep farming lands in the great basin.

State Highway 73 officially begins as a continuation of the Port Hills Road from Lyttelton (Highway 74) south of the city and encompasses the city's southern motorway, but the traditional beginning has been Yaldhurst Road in the south-west of Christchurch. The highway then leads through the suburbs of Yaldhurst and West Melton and meets the railway at Aylesbury, which it parallels as far as Springfield.

The original coach road between Yaldhurst and Sheffield was some distance to the north of the present road, closer to the Waimakariri River. Similarly in Westland the road went down the Arahura River for the last section to Hokitika rather than via the Taramakau route to Kumara. The first coach service was inaugurated by Cobb and Co. on 4 July 1865 and the first 36-hour journey to the West Coast in March 1866. The journey began in Christchurch which continued to be the starting point even after the railway was opened to Sheffield, and it was not until the railway was opened to Springfield that the starting point was changed to this terminus. The first hotel was built near Little Racecourse Hill and a second known as the "Malvern Arms" was built between Sheffield and Annat and used until 1874 when the railway was opened to Sheffield. As well as housing drinkers and travellers, religious services were held in it until the churches were built.

Sights of interest between Aylesbury and Springfield are basically those described in the chapter on the railway. After Springfield the road deviates away to the south of the railway via Porter's Pass, and does not meet it again until Cass.

In geographical order, features of interest in this section of road include:

Porter's Pass

Named after the family who took up the first Castle Hill run. An inn known as Riddle's Inn was established here in October 1865, containing 10 rooms, a 10 stalled stable and yards. The original road to Porter's Pass was intended only as a bridle path and was replaced by a new road in November 1871. At 945 metres above sea level, Porter's Pass is actually higher than Arthur's Pass, and is sometimes blocked by snow in the winter. The telegraph pole built here in the 1860s was for a while the highest in the country.

Lake Lyndon

A small lake near the junction of the Craigieburn, Torlesse and Big Ben ranges, 3 km west of Porter's Pass. The lake is sometimes frozen over in winter and used by ice-skaters. There is a day shelter and toilet block by the roadside. A "fair condition" road with several fords (sometimes closed in winter) leads from here to Lake Coleridge, 10 km away. Mount Lyndon rises to 1,475 metres from the western shoreline of the lake.

Porter Heights Ski Field

The turn-off is clearly marked and as the closest ski field to Christchurch enjoys great popularity in season with three T-bar tows with a total rise of 730 metres. There is equipment hire and accommodation facilities on the field.

Castle Hill

The name comes from the crop of limestone rocks which resemble the ruins of castle, worn smooth by the weather over the centuries. The five-room sheep station homestead is likewise made of limestone. A hotel was established here in 1865. Later in 1871 a new limestone block hotel with a Post Office was built opposite the present Castle Hill village. In 1881 a second story was added, making 28 rooms. With its first class accommodation and picturesque scenery it proved popular. It was gutted by fire in 1904 and not re-established. A conservation area reached before the Castle Hill Homestead contains the famous limestone rocks with foot access from the highway.

One early explorer, Rev. Charles Clarke, in **Rambles on the Golden** Coast described the Castle Hill rocks thus: "Late in the

The view looking east from the top of Porter's Pass.

afternoon we opened on a broad sunny valley and saw on a distant hillside an assemblage of rocks, some grouped like the buildings of a Cyclopean city deserted by its founders, some standing alone, stern and grim like sentries petrified at their posts; others again looking like the tombs of a colossal graveyard, or the circling seats of a vast amphitheatre; and further still huge groups and solitary masses like the gigantic monoliths of Stonehenge."

Castle Hill Village
A village established for holiday accommodation. The number of houses at the time of writing totalled approximately 60.

Mount Cheeseman Ski Field
The first ski club to be established was in 1929 at Mount Cheeseman on the Craigieburn Range. A 5.6 km road leads to the site of the Forest Lodge at an altitude of 1,000 metres, and at the 1,200 metre level is the Middle Hut dating from 1947 and further up again is the Top Lodge from 1950.

Cave Stream Scenic Reserve

This provides pleasant picnic spots near the highway as it approaches the Craigieburn saddle. The stream flows down to Broken River through a limestone cave which can be walked through at *low* level, a good flashlight and warm clothing being required. (A three-metre waterfall has to be negotiated.)

Craigieburn Forest Park

A signpost points out the turn-off to this large park covering 44,000 hectares which incorporates the more distant Avoca, Harper and Wilberforce forests. A privately run "Environmental Education Centre" has been situated 2 km from the turn-off. Information including pamphlets on the walks in the park is available from the Arthur's Pass visitor centre. Included in the park are the Broken River and Craigieburn Valley ski fields. Camp and picnic sites are at the " Craigieburn Picnic Area".

Broken River Ski Field

This field was developed in the years following World War II by members of the North Canterbury Ski Club and following the construction of a road up the valley of Cave Stream, the basin was first skied in 1952.

Flock Hill

The name of the first sheep station to occupy the Waimakariri Gorge, located to the south of Lake Pearson. The remains of the original 1857 cob cottage can be seen on the property. Today the station covers 14,000 hectares and farms deer cattle and sheep. The lodge on the property offers accommodation year round as well as a tearooms and restaurant for passers-by. Around here scenes were filmed for the movie *The Chronicles of Narnia: the Lion, the Witch and the Wardrobe* (2005).

Lake Pearson

Shaped like a figure of eight, this important habitat for waterfowl lies in a valley between Mount Manson (1,844 metres) at the northern end of the Craigieburn range and Purple Hill (1,679 metres). It was named after pioneer runholder Joseph Pearson who was the

The limestone rock formations of Castle Hill.

The confluence of Cave Stream and Broken River.
Flock Hill and the road around the hour-glass shaped Lake Pearson.

first European to explore the upper reaches of the Waimakariri River. Fishing for brown and rainbow trout is popular here.

Lake Grasmere
Likewise containing brown and rainbow trout but much smaller than Lake Pearson, this lake is surrounded by tussock covered hills about 3 km south-east of Cass. The lake is a wildlife refuge (power boating and shooting are prohibited) and a scenic reserve encompasses the beech forest on the eastern side. The name comes from the nearby sheep station.

Cass
A 16-room inn was established here in 1865 for coach passengers. Later in conjunction with the hotel, a store and blacksmith's shop was operated. As well there was a library and a racecourse and one of the attractions of the place was shooting wild cattle. The present day road passes about 700 metres from the Cass settlement which is situated in breakwind of trees. When the railway reached here, this became the coaching terminus and the station facilities were relatively elaborate. When railway staff were based here it was regarded as one of the least popular places to be stationed. The only vegetables that would grow were potatoes. There is a metalled side road leading to Craigieburn and Avoca (the original coach route) and there is fishing in Lake Sarah, accessible on the road, just over the railway crossing.

Goldney Saddle
After crossing a new bridge over the Cass River (opened in 1996) there follows an ascent between the mounds of Corner Knob (813 metres) and the Goldney Saddle (680 metres) before descending again near the junction of the Cass and Waimakariri Rivers, 3 km north-west of Cass. The Goldney Salle is named after the Goldney family who were early squatters in Canterbury. There is a turn-off here for the road to the Mount White Homestead which crosses the Waimakariri on a vehicle bridge to reach the foot of the 1,744 metre Mount Whiter, some distance eastwards down the Waimakariri River. This also gives access to the eastern side of Arthur's Pass National Park.

After rounding Corner Knob, the highway and railway travel alongside each other again for a few hundred metres before the railway crosses the Waimakariri River while the road continues along the south bank for some kilometres. After the road crosses the Waimakariri it travels up the west bank of the Bealey River, and the railway meets the road after its crossing of the Bealey and the two run side by side into Arthur's Pass.

Bealey

A settlement of holiday homes above the road was established once the Arthur's Pass township had outgrown its limits. There used to be a staging post and settlement on the shingle flats here. The accommodation house was the Glacier Hotel and named after the glacier at the source of the Waimakariri River. The one-time owner was a Mr O'Malley who took guided parties to the glacier and Kilmarnock Falls. There also used to be a telegraph office and police barracks when police were stationed here in the goldmining era. The old jail was used as a storehouse for the hotel for some years. A new hotel, again owned by an Irishman, was constructed and opened on 6 December 1990 which again offers a bar and accommodation for travellers.

Waimakariri Road Bridge

Before the building of this bridge in 1935-36, cars had to be towed through the river on top of a large horse wagon. There is parking area before the bridge providing for a tranquil picnicking spot. Exploration of the riverbank will reveal an old milestone near the water's edge marking the spot where coaches and cards used to ford the river. There is a grand view from here of the Waimakariri headwaters.

Klondyke Corner

In the initial excitement that followed the construction of a road over Arthur's Pass, a township mushroomed here and was known as the Bealey Township. Sir Julius von Haast in his **Geology of Canterbury and Westland** said, "On 5 October 1865 we reached the newly founded settlement of Bealey. Several houses have been constructed of logs or covered with weatherboards or zinc which together with a good array of tents indicates that a number of people have congregated there." At one stage the township numbered more than 100 inhabitants, while a considerable number of diggers and navvies who went to and fro made it their resting-place. Today virtually nothing remains to show where the town once stood apart from a few graves, although these are not obvious. It is a pleasant spot for picnicking and camping and a stone shelter plus fireplaces, tables and toilets are available here. The name is from that of a goldfield in Alaska.

Truggs Corner
Named after an early coach driver, Martin Trugg. Across the river is Mount O'Malley (1,692 metres) named after a one-time owner of the Bealey hotel.

Con's Flat
Named after Con McDavitt, an early roadman in the area. A fine view of the headwaters of the Mingha River can be seen here. Mount Oates (2,009 metres) towers above the head of the Mingha River valley.

Mingha River
Named after Mingha Wilson, the wife of the General Manager and Chief Engineer of the Midland Railway Company, Robert Wilson, this leads up to the 1,076 metre Goat Pass, on the other side of which is the Deception River, which will be seen at a point on the western side of the Alps from both the road and railway.

Arthur's Pass Village
The headquarters and visitor's centre of Arthur's Pass National Pass is situated here as well as a restaurant, public telephone, craft shop and café (Oscar's Haus) and a general store with a snack bar and petrol pump. (See the chapters on the railway and on stopovers).

McGrath's Creek
Named after a road contractor who built this section of the road when it was put through. The first road continued up the bank of the Bealey River and around to White's Bridge. A view of the Bridal Veil Falls can be seen here.

Above: The Glacier Hotel at Bealey in coaching days *ATL*
Below: Sometimes at Arthur's Pass a special treat may await in the form of a steam excursion train, here J1236 of the Mainline Steam Trust.

Jack's Hut
An old roadman's hut, visible from the road, now a privately owned holiday bach.

Rolleston Lookout
From here there is a magnificent view of Mount Rolleston (2275 metres), named after William Rolleston. The Goldney Glacier which can be seen below the ridge is permanent ice and snow.

Temple Basin Ski Field
A carpark and a steep foot track marks the route to the Temple Basin Ski Field. There is a good view of Mount Phipps (1,984 metres) and Mount Temple (1,893 metres) from here as well as of the Ribbon Falls on the parallel Twin Creek. The ski field was developed in the later 1920s when the Christchurch Ski Club was formed. The first hut was built in 1933 at an altitude of 1,400 metres. This field in 1948 had the first short ski tow in the country, powered by a small petrol engine. Today there are four ski tows with a combined vertical lift of 550 metres.

Dobson Monument
Erected in memory of Arthur Dudley Dobson who discovered the pass in March 1864 and who later became a member of the original park board. A plane table is also erected here which names peaks and points of interest in the area. The Dobson Nature Walks starts on the other side of the road.

Main Divide
A small roadside stone monument marks the border between Canterbury and Westland. At 929 metres this is actually slightly lower than Porter's Pass.

Goods Lift
The goods lift is used to carry supplies to the Temple Basin Ski Field. Some of the huts and ski tows in the basin can be seen from the road. In the days when stock was driven to the West Coast to feed the miners, the flat at the back of the shelter shed was used as a holding paddock where the animals were held overnight before continuing their journey down to the Arahura yards.

Lake Misery
In coaching days this was known as either Lake Misery or Lake Bright Eye. The lake drains into the Otira River by way of moraine seepage and with high rainfall can flood across the road.

Upper Otira Valley
A track to the Otira Valley starts at this point, which is one of the routes to climb Mount Rolleston.

Pegleg Creek
A certain Pegleg Charlie (who had a wooden leg) once had a hut by this bridge. He was supposed to be fossicking for gold, but in fact this was a blind for his trade of sly grogging and selling whisky to travellers over the pass.

Warnocks Knob
A beehive spur running from Mount Philistine (1,951 metres) into the Otira Gorge is a conspicuous feature of the view down the gorge. The "knob" is 1,168 metres. Surveyors for the Otira tunnel who erected a major trig point here named it after a one-time resident of Arthur's Pass.

Lookout
A twisting ascent used to take the road to the highest point, but this has been eliminated by the Otira Viaduct. Part of the road leading to what was known as Death Corner (after a coaching accident) now serves a lookout.

Otira Viaduct
Built to eliminate the notorious zig zag section of the road, which was in danger of being wiped out in the next major earthquake by the scree slides poised above it, this viaduct is one of the most impressive in the country. It consists of four spans on three piers, is eight metres wide and 440 metres long. It involved 5,000 cubic metres of concrete, 210 km of stressing wire and cost just under $25 million to build. The gradient is about 11%. Unfortunately the construction was not without a fatal accident. The viaduct was officially opened by the Prime Minister on 6 November 1999. Although the viaduct has removed the thrill of the zig zag section of the road, a good view of the Otira Gorge is still had.

Candy's Bend
Named after roadman Tom Candy who lived here in a hut, which was demolished in an earthquake in 1929. The bend has been eased considerably by roadworks accompanying the Otira viaduct construction.

Reid Falls
A waterfall which used to fall beside the road (and in wet weather sometimes across it); now carried in a chute over the road. Nearby there is a large shelter over the road against rock falls.

Starvation Point
Known originally as Starvation Corner, but it has been blasted away in recent decades. Fares were collected at this stage in the journey in coaching days; anyone who could not pay was left behind in this uninviting spot.

Wesley Creek
Those who venture up this very rugged creek will be rewarded with views of the highest falls in the park. John Wesley was in charge of construction of this section in 1866. Just beyond here there were

The Otira Viaduct.

hot springs at one-time, heralded by a strong smell of sulphur, but they were buried by a large slip.

Barrack Creek
The Rolleston River joins the Otira River at this point. The railway can be seen running along to the west entrance to the tunnel. A hotel named the George Hotel once stood on the flat. This was washed away in a flood and another hotel, the Otira Gorge Hotel, was built on the north-west side of the present road, just before reaching the Otira Bridge, some remains of which are still visible. The name Barrack Creek comes from police barracks that were once here. A large amount was spent on giving the police who manned these barracks training on catching bushrangers, but the gold escort over the gorge only made one journey, with less than one ounce of gold. A track leads from its mouth to the 1,649 metre Goat Hill.

The road and railway meet again above Otira and accompany each other as far as Jackson where State Highway 73 continues directly to the coast at Kumara Junction, while the railway winds north-west to Greymouth. Sights of interest between Otira and Jackson are described in the chapter on the railway.

The Avenue Scenic Reserve
Encountered just after the junction of the road leading to Inchbonnie.

Rocky Point
A scenic reserve is encountered a few kilometres along the road after rounding Rocky Point, opposite the Inchbonnie Bluff across the river. A side road leads to an airstrip.

Kumara
A township about 6 km east of Kumara Junction, best known as the home of one-time New Zealand Premier, Richard ("King Dick") Seddon. The site of his home here until 1895 is marked. The town grew as the main commercial centre for various gold diggings in the vicinity following the first strike of payable gold in July 1864 by

prospector Albert Hunt at Maori Point near the junction of the Greenstone and Taramakau Rivers. The name is corruption of "Kohimara", the local name of the flower of a noxious weed and has nothing to do with the name of New Zealand's sweet potato. The Kumara racecourse is about 1 km to the west of the town.

Kumara Junction

The end (or beginning) of Highway 73, 18 km south of Greymouth and 23 km north of Hokitika. Also one-time station on the Greymouth – Hokitika – (Ross) railway which is just beside the road at this point. On the way to Greymouth the Taramakau combined road/rail bridge is crossed, one of only six such bridges remaining in New Zealand.

A painting in the Arthur's Pass railway station showing the Cobb & Co stagecoach crossing the Otira River in the 19th century.

Stop-Overs

Christchurch

Detailed information on sights of interest and things to do in Christchurch will be found in general travel guides that are regularly published. For those with an interest in historic transport, however, the following are places to include on an itinerary:

Canterbury Museum
Located on Rolleston Avenue, this contains exhibits from the old coaching days, shop fronts and general information on the region. Open daily between 9.00 am – 5.00 pm.

Ferrymead Historic Park
Reached by travelling towards Summer and then turning off at Bridle Path Road, this contains among other things an operating electric tramway with restored tramcars from different municipal bodies; some preserved aircraft; an old time village; an operating railway with several preserved steam locomotives and old style passenger cars; and a hall containing a large collection of vintage fire trucks. Open daily 10.00 am- 4.30 pm. The tramways are operated daily and the railway on weekends and public holidays.

Yaldhurst Transport Museum
Situated off State Highway 73 opposite the Yaldhurst hotel, this contains a variety of horse-drawn and mechanised transport vehicles, as well as old amusement machines in penny arcades.

Air Force World
Situated at the former Wigram airbase with entry from the main south road, this contains a fascinating display of New Zealand's military aviation history. Open daily 10.00 am – 5.00 pm.

Arthur's Pass

This is the fourth largest of New Zealand's 13 national parks, covering about 100,000 hectares, two thirds of it in Canterbury, and one-third in Westland.

The park offers one of the easiest accesses to the alpine zone along the main divide and it has the northern-most glaciers in the South Island. The highest mountain in the park is Mount Murchison (2,408 metres), which is at the headwaters of the White River, a tributary of the Waimakariri River near its headwaters.

There are several tramping routes, details on which will be found in the park handbook and in the set of route guides. For those preferring day walk, there are also several possibilities, which are likewise to be found in information available at the park Visitor's Centre. A few of these include:

Historic Walk around Arthur's Pass Village

A pamphlet available from the park headquarters provides a guide to historic sites around the village, at which historic photographs have been mounted (1½ -hours round trip).

Coach Road

A short 15 minute walking track follows a section of the old coach road near the Bealey rail bridge. It starts from Greyneys Shelter and climbs above the present road, levelling out on the overgrown coach road with its hand laid stone walls (20 minute around trip).

Devil's Punchbowl Falls Walk

This well known waterfall, used to power a generating station during the drilling of the Otira tunnel (the site of which is still visible), can be seen from a number of points on tracks leading to the ridge-lines in the valley. A track from the northern end of the village crosses the Bealey and Punchbowl Rivers and climbs through the beech forest to the base of these spectacular falls (80 minute round trip).

Bridal Veil Walk

From the Bealey River footbridge at the northern end of the township you can walk through the beech forest on the eastern side of the valley higher up The track reaches a lookout above the Bridal Veil Steam after 30 minutes. There is a short drop to the stream and a climb from the stream bed to a more level section, board-walked in places, to the road. The start of the Bealey Valley Track is slightly further up the road from where this track comes out (2-hours return).

Greymouth

Sights of interest in Greymouth include the new anti-flood wall into which the former railway signal box is now half-submerged, the old and new Cobden rail bridges, and the fishing boat wharves near the outflow of the Grey River into the sea. Half day excursions include the Brunner industrial site as well as:

Rewanui

The site of a former coal mine, which finally closed in 1985. In steam days it was a mecca for rail enthusiasts who used to watch Ww and WE tank locomotives fight their way up the 5.4 km on a 1 in 26 gradient from Dunollie to the mine site. The gradient was the second steepest on NZR after the Rimutaka Incline. Excursion passenger trains were run up to the mine site until 1984. A preservation group was formed following the closure of the mine, but much new work was created for it by a major landslide on 17 September 1988 which destroyed several buildings and bridges. Rewanui is reached by following the Westport highway as far as Runanga, 7 km away, and then following the signposts pointing out Rewanui and Dunollie to the right.

Shantytown

Some 13 km south of Greymouth via Paroa and Rutherglen, is a recreated goldmining township of the 1860s which appeared in several locations on the West Coast, nearly all now having disappeared with only a few ruins to tell what was once there. Some buildings, such as the church from Notown and the Coronation Hall from Ross are original, but most are reconstructions from original plans. Two vintage steam locomotives, an 0-6-0T modified F type locomotive from 1896 and named **Kaitangata**, ex- The Kaitangata Coal Company in South Otago, and an 0-4-4-0T Climax locomotive from 1913, ex- Ellis and Burnand's tramway near Ongarue, make short trips into the bush to old Chinese workings and gold seekers can pan for gold. Cobb and Co. stagecoaches make trips in the summer. Open daily.